SCARLETT JOHANSSON

BY MARY BLECKWEHL

AMICUS LEARNING

Inspire is published by
Amicus Learning, an imprint of Amicus
P.O. Box 227
Mankato, MN 56002
www.amicuspublishing.us

Editor: Ana Brauer
Series Designer: Kathleen Petelinsek
Book Designer and Photo Researcher: Emily Dietz

Library of Congress Cataloging-in-Publication Data
Names: Bleckwehl, Mary E. author
Title: Scarlett Johansson / by Mary Bleckwehl.
Description: Mankato, MN : Amicus Learning, 2026. | Series: Inspire | Includes bibliographical references and index. | Audience term: Children | Audience: Ages 5-9 | Audience: Grades 2-3 | Summary: "From child actor to Marvel superhero! This engaging biography explores how Scarlett Johansson rose to fame, starring in *Lost in Translation*, becoming Black Widow in *The Avengers*, and leading blockbuster films. Includes table of contents, glossary, further resources, and index" — Provided by publisher.
Identifiers: LCCN 2025011922 (print) | LCCN 2025011923 (ebook) | ISBN 9798892008655 library binding | ISBN 9798892009317 paperback | ISBN 9798892009973 ebook
Subjects: LCSH: Johansson, Scarlett, 1984—Juvenile literature | Motion picture actors and actresses—Biography—United States—Juvenile literature | LCGFT: Biographies
Classification: LCC PN2287.J575 B56 2026 (print) | LCC PN2287.J575 (ebook) | DDC 791.4302/8092 [B]—dc23/eng/20250324
LC record available at https://lccn.loc.gov/2025011922
LC ebook record available at https://lccn.loc.gov/2025011923

Photo Credits: Associated Press/Vianney Le Caer, cover; Alamy Stock Photo/Capital Pictures, 20, Collection Christophel, 15, kpa Publicity Stills, 6, Marvel Studios, 4, Pictorial Press, 10; Getty Images/ANGELA WEISS, 12, Herbert Dorfman, 17, Jeff Gritchen/MediaNews Group/Orange County Register, 18, MEGA, 14, Mike Marsland, 9, Paolo Blocco, 21, Steve Granitz, 13, Steve Zak Photography, 16; Shutterstock/pearleyes, 19

Printed in the United States of America

Table of Contents

Scarlett Johansson is famous for playing Natasha Romanoff (Black Widow) in superhero movies.

Lights! Camera! Action!

Scarlett Johansson leaps onto the movie set. She spins, kicks, and sends her enemies flying. Her fight looks real. It's what an action star does to make a movie come to life. Scarlett Johansson is an American actress.

Young Johansson got her start in the movie *North* (1994).

Born to Shine

Johansson was born in New York City. Her family didn't have much money. That didn't stop her from dreaming. She wanted to be in movies. She started by **auditioning** for commercials. At nine years old, her dream came true. She made her **debut** in the movie *North* (1994).

Breakout Roles

As a child, Johansson had small movie parts. But her lead role in *The Horse Whisperer* (1998) brought attention. This led to adult parts. Her breakout role was in *Lost in Translation* (2003).

In 2004, Johansson won a **BAFTA** award for *Lost in Translation.*

Johansson's first superhero movie was *Iron Man 2* (2010).

Becoming a Superhero

Johansson starred in nine **Marvel** movies as Black Widow. This is the role she's best known for. She took stunt training to prepare. Black Widow inspired girls to be brave and take risks.

A GOOD HAIR DAY!
Johansson dyed her hair red to play Black Widow.

A Hollywood Star

Johansson's success earned her a star on the Hollywood Walk of Fame in 2012. Some of her costars from *The Avengers* (2012) cheered her on at her award ceremony. Her star tells the world that dreams do come true.

DID YOU KNOW?
Johansson was **nominated** for two Oscars in 2020. She was one of 12 actors who were nominated twice in the same year.

Johansson and her *Avengers* costar Jeremy Renner pose with her Hollywood star.

Johansson directed her first movie, *Eleanor the Great*, in 2025.

Beyond Acting

Fans know Johansson as an award-winning actress. But her talents are many. She directs movies and sings. She's been in music videos and ads. The star had a sneaker line. Now she has a skincare line.

FUN WITH VOICES

Johansson was the voice of a rock-singing porcupine in *Sing* (2016) and a robot in *Transformers One* (2024).

Inspiration

Johansson's mom and grandmother wanted her to follow her dreams. But her acting inspiration came from Judy Garland. Johansson and Garland were both young when they started acting.

TWINS!
Johansson has a twin brother named Hunter. He is an actor, too.

Judy Garland is best known for playing Dorothy in *The Wizard of Oz* (1939).

In 2019, Johansson and Robert Downey Jr. donated $5 million to support children's hospitals.

Giving Back

On top of a busy career, Johansson finds time for others. Her family needed help to buy food when she was young. Supporting **charities** like Feeding America is important to her now. She believes kids can do amazing things when they are well fed.

DID YOU KNOW?
Johansson has donated more than 2,000 pairs of shoes to Soles4Souls.

Looking Ahead

Dreams and hard work made Johansson a successful actress. Her big heart helps feed families and their dreams. What new dreams does this superstar have? Maybe she will direct a blockbuster. Whatever comes next, fans can't wait to see.

DINO DREAMS
Johansson dreamed of being in a *Jurassic Park* movie. That came true in 2025 with *Jurassic World Rebirth.*

TIME **magazine named Johansson one of the most influential people in the world in 2021 and 2025.**

SUPER STATS

SCARLETT INGRID JOHANSSON

Birthday: November 22, 1984

Birthplace: New York City, NY

Children: 2

Major Film Roles: *The Horse Whisperer* (1998), *Lost in Translation* (2003), *The Avengers* (2012), *Marriage Story* (2019), *Jurassic World Rebirth* (2025)

MAJOR AWARDS

BAFTA Winner: 2004

Tony Award: 2010

People's Choice Female Movie Star: 2021

Academy Award Nominations: 2

Golden Globes Nominations: 5

GLOSSARY

audition A tryout for a performing part.

BAFTA The British Academy of Film and Television Arts. BAFTA gives awards to the best actors, movies, and TV shows.

charity A group or organization that helps people in need.

debut A person's first time performing.

Marvel Referring to movies that feature Marvel Comics characters.

nominate To choose as a candidate for office or an award.

READ MORE

Behling, Steve. **Who's Who in the Marvel Universe.** New York, NY: Marvel Press, 2020.

Kawa, Katie. **Scarlett Johansson is Black Widow.** Milwaukee, WI: Gareth Stevens Publishing, 2019.

ON THE WEB

AstroSafe
https://www.astrosafe.co/article/scarlett_johansson

Britannica Kids
https://kids.britannica.com/students/article/Scarlett-Johansson/610085

Kiddle: Scarlett Johansson
https://kids.kiddle.co/Scarlett_Johansson

INDEX

About the Author

Mary Bleckwehl is a children's author who loves cookie dough and talking to kids. She is happiest when she is biking and exploring new places. Mary lives in Minnesota with her husband and monster dog. Check out her books at marybleckwehl.com.

KIT CONNOR

BY JOANNE MATTERN

AMICUS LEARNING

Inspire is published by
Amicus Learning, an imprint of Amicus
P.O. Box 227
Mankato, MN 56002
www.amicuspublishing.us

Editor: Ana Brauer
Series Designer: Kathleen Petelinsek
Book Designer and Photo Researcher: Emily Dietz

Library of Congress Cataloging-in-Publication Data
Names: Mattern, Joanne, 1963- author
Title: Kit Connor / by Joanne Mattern.
Description: Mankato, MN : Amicus Learning, 2026. | Series: Inspire | Includes bibliographical references and index. | Audience: Ages 5–9 | Audience: Grades 2–3 | Summary: "From child actor to breakout star! Discover how Kit Connor went from roles in *Get Santa* and *Rocketman* to winning hearts as Nick Nelson in *Heartstopper*. This engaging biography includes a table of contents, glossary, further resources, and index"—Provided by publisher.
Identifiers: LCCN 2025011924 (print) | LCCN 2025011925 (ebook) | ISBN 9798892008624 library binding | ISBN 9798892009287 paperback | ISBN 9798892009942 ebook
Subjects: LCSH: Connor, Kit, 2004—Juvenile literature | Motion picture actors and actresses—United States—Biography—Juvenile literature | LCGFT: Biographies
Classification: LCC PN2287.C5816 M38 2026 (print) | LCC PN2287.C5816 (ebook) | DDC 791.4302/8092 [B]—dc23/eng/20250325
LC record available at https://lccn.loc.gov/2025011924
LC ebook record available at https://lccn.loc.gov/2025011925

Photo Credits: Alamy Stock Photo/Album, 14, Collection Christophel, 10, NurPhoto, 4, Pictorial Press, 19; Associated Press/Jae C. Hong, cover; Getty Images/Bruce Glikas, 20, Danny Martindale, 8, Dave Benett, 17, Karwai Tang, 7; IMAGO/Everett Collection, 13; Shutterstock/Soonios Pro, 12, veryonephoto Studio, 15; Playbill Inc/unknown, 21

Printed in the United States of America